POP SONGS

THE VERY BEST

Wise Publications
London / New York / Paris / Sydney / Copenhagen / Madrid

Exclusive Distributors:

Music Sales Limited
8/9 Frith Street,
London W1D 3JB, England.

Music Sales Pty Limited
120 Rothschild Avenue,
Rosebery, NSW 2018,
Australia.

Order No. AM975777
ISBN 0-7119-9715-2
This book © Copyright 1997, 2002 by Wise Publications.

Compiled by Peter Evans.
Photographs courtesy of London Features International.

Printed in the United Kingdom by
Printwise (Haverhill) Limited, Suffolk.

Your Guarantee of Quality:
As publishers, we strive to produce every book
to the highest commercial standards.
This book has been carefully designed to minimise
awkward page turns and to make playing from it a real pleasure.
Particular care has been given to specifying acid-free, neutral-sized paper
made from pulps which have not been elemental chlorine bleached.
This pulp is from farmed sustainable forests and
was produced with special regard for the environment.
Throughout, the printing and binding have been planned to ensure
a sturdy, attractive publication which should give years of enjoyment.
If your copy fails to meet our high standards,
please inform us and we will gladly replace it.

www.musicsales.com

A Whiter Shade Of Pale

Procol Harum

Words & Music by Keith Reid & Gary Brooker.
© Copyright 1967 by Onward Music Limited, 11 Uxbridge Street, London W8.
All Rights Reserved. International Copyright Secured.

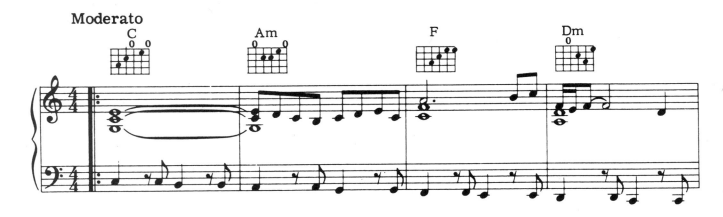

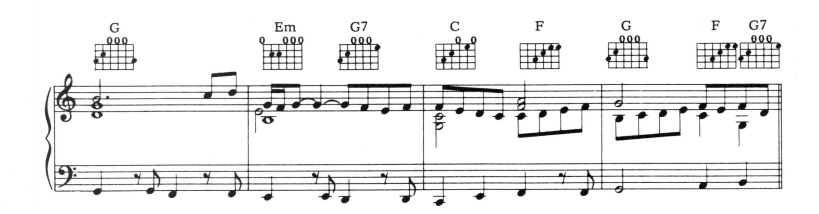

We skipped the light fan-dan-go   And turned cartwheels 'cross the
She said, "There is   no   rea-son,   And the   truth is ___ plain to

floor._
see.",_

I was feel-ing kind of sea-sick,
But I wan-dered through my playing cards

But the crowd called out for more,
And would not_ let her be.

The room was humming har-der
One of six-teen vest-al vir-gins

As the cei-ling flew a - way._
Who were lea-ving for the coast,_

When we called out for a - no - ther drink
And al-tho' my eyes were o - pen

The wai-ter brought a tray,— And so it was _____ that la-ter
They might just as well been closed,

As the mil-ler told his tale,— That her face at first just

ghostly, Turned a whi-ter _____ shade of pale._____ pale._____

Careless Whisper

George Michael

Words & Music by George Michael & Andrew Ridgeley.
© Copyright 1984 Morrison Leahy Music Limited, 1 Star Street, London W2.

I feel so__ un - sure__
Time can nev - er mend__
To - night the mu - sic seems so loud,__ I

__ wish that we__ could lose this crowd, may - be it's bet - ter this way, if we'd

as I take your hand__ and lead you
the care - less whis - per

to the dance floor; as the mu-sic dies_
of a good friend; to the heart and mind_
hurt each oth-er with the things we want to say._ We could have been_ so good to-geth - er, we

some-thing in your eyes_ calls to mind a sil - ver screen_ and
ig-nor-ance is kind_ there's no com - fort in the truth_
could have lived_ this dance for ev - er, but now who's gon - na dance with

you're its sad good - bye.
pain is_ all you'll find._
me. Please dance._ I'm nev - er gon - na dance a - gain,_

guil - ty feet have got_ no rhy-thm, though it's ea - sy to pre-tend,_ I know you're not_ a fool._ I

8

should have known bet-ter than to cheat a friend, and waste a chance that I've been gi-ven, so I'm nev-er gon-na dance a-gain_ the way I dance_with you.____

way I dance_with you, oh.___

way I dance_with you.___

Ad lib. to fade

9

He Ain't Heavy...He's My Brother

The Hollies

Words by Bob Russell. Music by Bobby Scott.
© Copyright 1969 by Harrison Music Corporation, USA & Jenny Music.
Chelsea Music Publishing Company Limited, 70 Gloucester Place, London W1H 4AJ/Jenny Music.
All Rights Reserved. International Copyright Secured.

la-den___ at all, ___ I'm la-den___ with sad-ness___ that

ev-'ry - one's heart is-n't filled ___ with the glad-ness ___ of

love _____ for one an - o - ther. _____ It's a long, long

D.S. al ⊕ 𝄋

How Deep Is Your Love

Bee Gees

Words & Music by Barry Gibb, Robin Gibb & Maurice Gibb.
© Copyright 1977 Gibb Brothers Music.
All Rights Reserved. International Copyright Secured.

Moderately

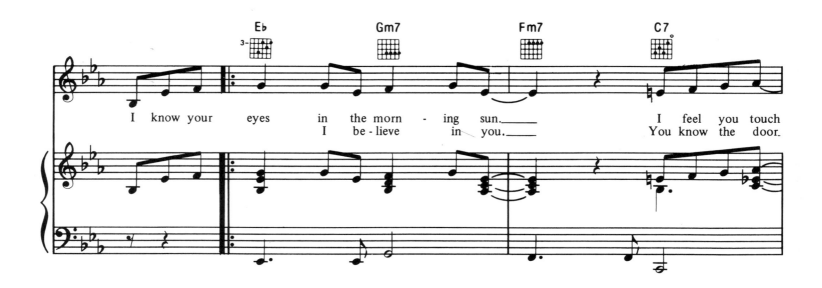

I know your eyes in the morn - ing sun._____ I feel you touch
I be - lieve in you._____ You know the door.

_____ me in the pour - ing rain._____ And the mo - ment that you wan - der far_____
to my ver - y soul._____ You're the light _____ in my deep - est, dark

If You Don't Know Me By Now

Simply Red

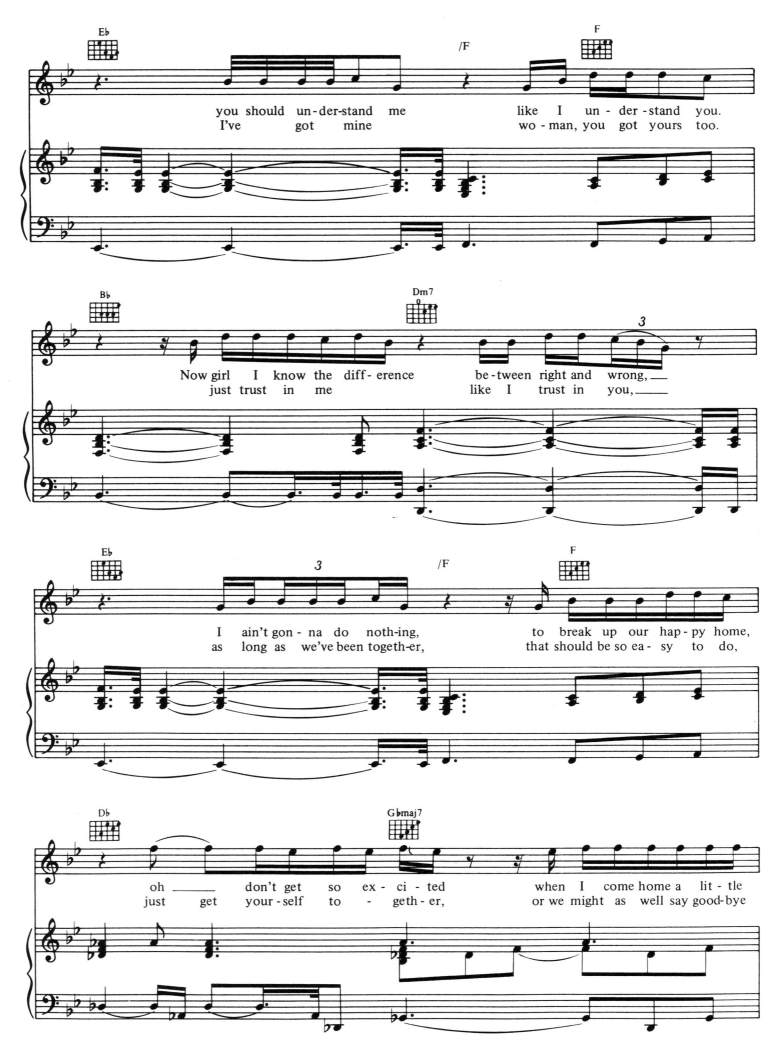

you should un-der-stand me like I un-der-stand you.
I've got mine wo-man, you got yours too.

Now girl I know the diff-erence be-tween right and wrong, ___
just trust in me like I trust in you, ___

I ain't gon-na do noth-ing, to break up our hap-py home,
as long as we've been togeth-er, that should be so ea-sy to do,

oh ___ don't get so ex-ci-ted when I come home a lit-tle
just get your-self to - geth-er, or we might as well say good-bye

late at night 'cause we on-ly act like child-ren   when we ar-gue, fuss and fight.
what good is a love af -   fair,   when you can't see eye to eye.

If you don't know me by now,___ you will nev-er nev-er nev-er know me   ooh.___

If you don't know me by now,___ you will nev-er nev-er nev-er know me   ooh.___

If you don't know me by now, ___ you will nev-er nev-er nev-er know me,   ooh.

If Not For You

Bob Dylan

be no-where at all. Oh! __ What would I __ do, __ If not __ for you. __

If not for you, __

Win - ter would

If You Leave Me Now

Chicago

Words & Music by Peter Cetera.
© Copyright 1976 BMG Songs Incorporated, USA.
BMG Music Publishing Limited, Bedford House, 69-79 Fulham High Street, London SW6 for the UK & Eire.
This arrangement © Copyright 1997 BMG Music Publishing Limited.
All Rights Reserved. International Copyright Secured.

If you leave__ me now__ you'll take a-way__ the big - gest part __ of me. __

Bmaj7   G#m7   D#m7

Ooh. _____ no, __ ba - by, please ____ don't go. __

G#m7 Csus4   F#   B   G#m7 C#7

Ooh, ____ girl, __   I've   got   to   have   you   by
Sweet __ ma - ma,   I   just   got   to   have ____ your

F#   B   G#m7   C#7   F#

Repeat and fade

my   side. _____
love   in ____ side. ____

Ooh, __

B   G#m7   C#7   F#   B

Tears In Heaven

Eric Clapton

VERSE 2:
Would you hold my hand
If I saw you in heaven?
Would you help me stand
If I saw you in heaven?
I'll find my way
Through night and day,
'Cause I know I just can't stay
Here in heaven.

VERSE 3: (D.S.)

Instrumental solo — 8 bars

Beyond the door
There's peace, I'm sure;
And I know there'll be no more
Tears in heaven.

VERSE 4: (D.S.)
Would you know my name
If I saw you in heaven?
Would you be the same
If I saw you in heaven?
I must be strong
And carry on,
'Cause I know I don't belong
Here in heaven.

One Moment In Time

Whitney Houston

The Lady In Red

Chris de Burgh

1. I've nev-er seen you look-ing so love-ly as you did to-night,
   nev-er seen you look-ing so gor-geous as you did to-night,

I've nev-er seen you shine so bright,
I've nev-er seen you shine so bright,

mm mm mm mm.
you were a-maz-ing.

I've
I've

never seen so ma - ny men ask _____ you if you want-ed to dance, _____
nev - er seen so ma - ny peo - ple want to be there _____ by your side, _____

_____ they're look-ing for a lit - tle ro - mance,
_____ and when you turned to me and smiled, _____ it

giv - en half _____ a chance, and I have
took my breath a - way, _____ and I have

nev - er seen that dress you're wear - ing, or the
nev - er had _____ such a feel - ing, such a

there's no - bo - dy here, ____

it's just you and me, ____ it's where I wan - na be,

but I hard - ly know ____

this beau - ty by my side, ____

The Long And Winding Road

The Beatles

Words & Music by John Lennon & Paul McCartney.
© Copyright 1970 Northern Songs.
All Rights Reserved. International Copyright Secured.

The Wind Beneath My Wings

Bette Midler

Words & Music by Jeff Silbar & Larry Henley.
© Copyright House Of Gold Music Incorporated & Bobby Goldsboro Music Incorporated, USA.
Warner Chappell Music Limited, 129 Park Street, London W1.
All Rights Reserved. International Copyright Secured.

Am(add B)   D   B/D#

I nev - er once__ heard you com - plain.

Em   C   G   D/F# D

Did you ev - er know__ that you're my__ he - ro,

Em   C   G   D/F# C/E D

and ev - 'ry - thing__ I'd like to be?

Em   C   G   D/F# D

I can fly high - er than an ea - gle,__

'cause you are the wind___ be-neath my wings.

It might have ap-peared___ to go un-

no - ticed that I've got it all___ here in my

heart.

I want you to know___ I know the

48

truth: I would be noth-

in'   with - out   you.

Coda

wings.   You are the wind__

___ be - neath my__ wings.

This Guy's In Love With You

Herb Alpert

You see ___ this guy, ___ this guy's in love with you. ___

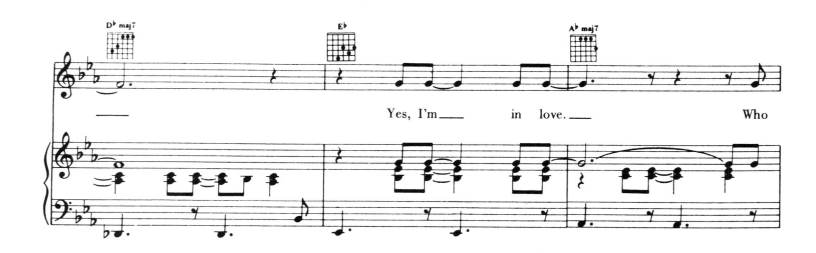

___ Yes, I'm ___ in love. ___ Who

let my heart keep break-ing, 'cause I need _ your love. _

I want _ your love. _

Say you're _ in love, in love with this

guy. _____ If not, I'll just die. _

Unchained Melody

The Righteous Brothers

Music by Alex North. Words by Hy Zaret.
© Copyright 1955 Frank Music Corporation, USA.
Published & Administered by MPL Communications Limited.
All Rights Reserved. International Copyright Secured.

What's Love Got To Do With It

Tina Turner

Words & Music by Graham Lyle & Terry Britten.
© Copyright 1984 Good Single Limited and Myaxe Music Limited.
Rondor Music (London) Limited, 10a Parsons Green, London SW6 (50%)/Warner Chappell Music Limited, 129 Park Street, London W1 (50%).

Verse 2:
It may seem to you
That I'm acting confused
When you're close to me.
If I tend to look dazed,
I read it some place;
I've got cause to be.
There's a name for it,
There's a phrase that fits,
But whatever the reason,
You do it for me.

(To Chorus)

Where Do Broken Hearts Go?

Whitney Houston

Words & Music by Frank Wildhorn & Chuck Jackson.
© Copyright 1985 Scaramanga Music/Rare Blue Music Incorporated/Baby Love Music, USA.
Rights administered in the World excluding USA & Canada by Chrysalis Music Limited, The Old Phoenix Brewery, Bramley Road, London SW10.
All Rights Reserved. International Copyright Secured.

on - ly things I learned   is that I | need you des - p'rate - ly.
mat - ter now I try,   you're | al - ways on __ my mind. __ So

here I __ am, __   and | can you please __ tell __ me: __   oh __

Chorus:

Where do bro-ken hearts go; | can they find their __ way __ home | back to the o - pen arms of a

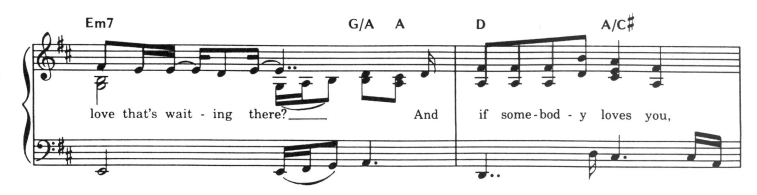

love that's wait - ing there? __   And | if some-bod - y loves you,

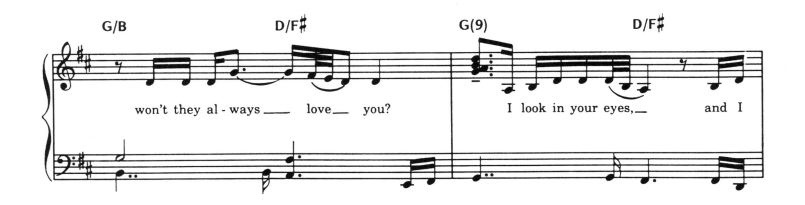

won't they al - ways ___ love ___ you?   I look in your eyes, ___ and I

1. know that you ___ still care ___ for | **2.** know that you ___ still care ___ for me. ___ And

Bridge:

now that I _____ am here with you, ___   I'll ___ nev-er let you go. ___ I

look in-to ___ your ___ eyes, ___ and now I   know,   now I   know.

Wonderwall

Oasis

Words & Music by Noel Gallagher

To-day is gon-na be the day that they're gon-na throw it back to you,—

by now you should-'ve some-how re-al-ised what you got-ta do.—

I don't be - lieve— that an - y - bo - dy feels the way I do— a - bout you now.—

1. Back - beat the word was on the street that the fi - re in your heart is out.—
(Verse 2 see block lyric)

I'm sure you've heard it all be - fore but you nev - er real - ly had a doubt.—

There are ma - ny things_ that I_ would like to say to you_ but I don't know how,_

{be - cause} {I said}

may - be_ you're gon - na be the one that

saves me,_ and af - ter all_

may - be _____ you're gon - na be the one that

(Continue as instr.)

Repeat 7 times

saves me, _____ you're gon - na be the one that

Verse 2:
Today was gonna be the day
But they'll never throw it back to you
By now you should've somehow
Realised what you're not to do
I don't believe that anybody
Feels the way I do
About you now.

And all the roads that lead you there were winding
And all the lights that light the way are blinding
There are many things that I would like to say to you
But I don't know how.

Your Song

Elton John

Words & Music by Elton John and Bernie Taupin.
© Copyright 1969 for the World by Dick James Music Limited, 47 British Grove, London W4.
All Rights Reserved. International Copyright Secured.

I'm don't — have much   mon-ey, _____ but,   boy, if I   did, _____
know — it's not   much but it's — the   best I can   do, _____
But the sun's been quite   kind _____ is   while I wrote this song, _____
An-y-way — the   thing _____ is   what I real-ly   mean, _____

I'd buy — a big house   where _____   we both could live.
My gift is my song   and _____
It's for peo-ple like you,   that _____   keep it — turned on.
Yours are the   sweet-est   eyes _____

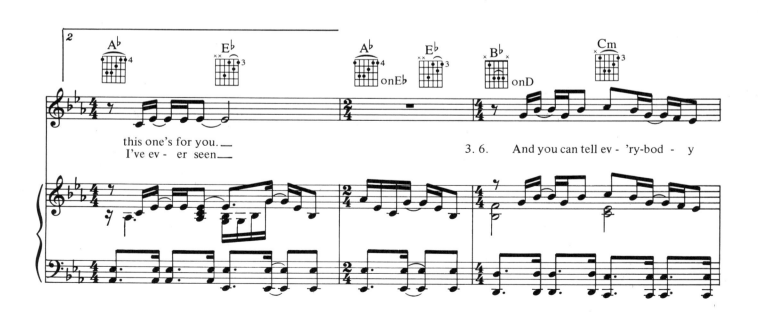

this one's for you. _____
I've ev - er seen _____

3. 6.   And you can tell ev - 'ry-bod - y

7.8. I hope you don't mind, __ I hope you don't mind __ that I put __ down in __ words, How

won- der- ful life is __ while you're __ in __ the world. __

you're __ in __ the world. ___

Yesterday

The Beatles

Words & Music by John Lennon & Paul McCartney.
© Copyright 1965 Northern Songs.

Moderately

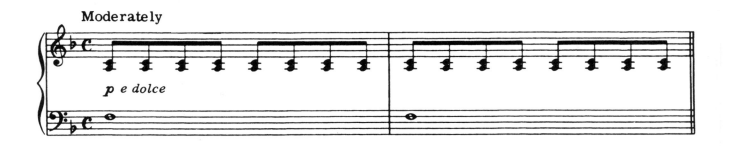

Yes - ter - day,   all my trou - bles seemed so   far a - way

Now it looks as though they're here   to   stay____   Oh